Prologue for
the Age of Consequence

Garth Martens

PROLOGUE FOR THE AGE OF CONSEQUENCE

ANANSI

This edition published in 2014 by
House of Anansi Press Inc.
110 Spadina Avenue, Suite 801 Toronto, ON, M5V 2K4
Tel. 416-363-4343 Fax 416-363-1017
www.houseofanansi.com

Distributed in Canada by
HarperCollins Canada Ltd.
1995 Markham Road Scarborough, ON, M1B 5M8
Toll free tel. 1-800-387-0117.

Distributed in the United States by
Publishers Group West
1700 Fourth Street Berkeley, CA 94710,
Toll free tel. 1-800-788-3123.

House of Anansi Press is committed to protecting our natural environment. As part of our efforts, the interior of this book is printed on paper made from second-growth forests and is acid-free.

18 17 16 15 14   1 2 3 4 5

Library and Archives Canada Cataloguing in Publication

Martens, Garth, author
Prologue for the age of consequence / Garth Martens.

Issued in print and electronic formats.
ISBN 978-1-77089-810-3 (bound).—ISBN 978-1-77089-319-1 (pbk.).—
ISBN 978-1-77089-320-7 (pdf)

I. Title.

PS8626.A76853M67 2014   C811.6   C2013-907025-7   C2013-907026-5

Library of Congress Control Number: 2013918886

Cover design: Brian Morgan
Text design and typesetting: Brian Morgan.

 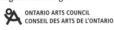

We acknowledge for their financial support of our publishing program the Canada Council for the Arts, the Ontario Arts Council, and the Government of Canada through the Canada Book Fund.

Printed and bound in Canada

For my father.

Contents

Prologue

Forget where you were going. The Whitemud, the Yellowhead, air warping from the cranked-down window through the truck, lead you out the tourist district, past tall townhouses, their vinyl yellows, greens, blues, stacked as if to keep you out. Through the overpass these give way to the concrete silo, a rail station, canola, wheat. Turn right onto a road that doesn't quite exist. It aims someplace, but won't make it through the mud. Scrapers and bulldozers, straining on caterpillar tread, carve hills at either side, mounds of soil stinking and black. Semi-trucks flank the route, drivers rushing to relieve their freight. Snagged in branches of black poplar and tamarack fronting the road, bag after bag is blown tight, the plastic wrinkled or stretched, mask-like. Cresting wooded slopes, you approach the site and the sun burns, foiling behind black thundercloud, molten like the light of a welder's tool. Nylon camping tents, hundreds along the ditches and clearings, streaked with scum, flare in the gusts. Men who have sailed every fjord or hunted every animal for a little pay have come here now with their many languages. They pack tylenol, meat, razors, coffee, news, migrating from trailers to their tents. Women wait for them, backs to the corrugated siding, smoke trailing from their nostrils. Think ahead to the bonfire at night. The sky that fills with a monument of flies, em-bered leaves, voices lit with whiskey. It is dark when you reach the excavation and you don't know if the road starts or ends here. If it's abutment, chimera, hole.

Everything That's Yours

It comes from the highway to the house,
from the frost on the seeds
and the station and the dream.

It comes from the bus
and the strangers in their sleep,
aspens like wicks in a flame.

It comes from the bird and the bird's chain.

♦

It comes from a country singer's voice,
ashes in the air.

Are they ashes, moths?
You can't say.

Everything that's yours,
a jar of receipts, the yellow ceiling,
a scale that counts your weight.

♦

It comes from oil on your plate,
a streak of gristle you cut
away and cut and cut.

♦

It comes from your son's mute steps
through the house.

From the neighbour's truck
and the cuffs of his eyes.
From the window overnight.

·

It comes from the purge
at the sink.

Ceramic tiles, the next drink.

·

It comes from the chattering needle
of a sewing machine.

The radio at the prompt.

Does your hand roll in
like a snailshell? Like a sickle?

·

It comes from the bath and the candle,
the woman and the cloth,
steam as it curls from her skin.

It comes before a question.

Are her eyes made up
or what?

Is it you we're talking about?

It comes from someone else's hand,
the drugs that let her sleep,
just go to sleep.

·

It comes from the understory of a ring,
the name on a knife,
from the horse in the yard and the horse before light.

Is it a tool for digging? A freewheeling hinge?

It comes from God in the oven,
panic in the sky.

·

It comes from the horse asking, When?
From spokes of a wheel, cigarette filters,
your son or the window asking.

It doesn't come from you,
it can never come from you,
the trees are burning
and the other hand, reluctantly,
takes the weight.

Inheritance

i.

The motor-oil seep of it. The sawdust sheen.
That first forage of his father's garage.

Plucked from a pocket, his toy soldier
sniped among the drill-bits,
swiped across horizons from a knot-hole.

He took a slim serrated thing in hand.
Drop that! His father
caught his wrist. The blade clattered.

ii.

He didn't shout again. It unnerved him,
how the boy shook silently.

He struck apart the old wood crate,
stays cracking on concrete.
Most landed near his feet. His boy
stole what he could, hid it behind the shed.

iii.

The boy dragged out the great river with a twig.
Erected a gaunt fortress of root, mud, and splintered stave.
Named it Belle Rive after his father's.

Aspens withered upright along the bank.
The water's transit cut the soil as it rose
sopping the base so it crumbled.

He could hear the hammer's hook, its reach and wrench.
The crate caved inward with each blow.

iv.

Before the tower sank within itself,
ebbing in the gorged river, he pressed
a toy figure where the earth was soft,
buried it with a fingertip, closed it under dark.

Inheritance II

The boy swept dust for a dollar.
The Boss's son,
he wanted to please,
captured insects from the heap
leggy in the choleric particulate air.

The boy was short at seven
but mercurial
clever in boyhood.
He tried for the
height of a door-frame,
the broken hang of a bulb.
Quick form of any
vessel he was tipped into,
garbage can, basement, closet,
his mother's burrwood box.

At lunch Big Iain brought an iced espresso.
The boy said, Let me.
He shot it back in his throat.
The men applauded.
So the boy was loud.
He fingered their tools,
he dropped them.
He threw a plastic lid at Iain's head.
The men said, Dampen down.
But no. He borrowed pride.
He echoed slurs.
He could not be quiet.
The men said, Still. Be still.
He could not.

He cupped a seventh
grasslegger in a glass.

Men, insect, each like that schoolyard trick
of the paper clip, an elastic,
wound in a card.
Nervy jumpers enveloped in a jar.

He tried to please,
to twist his knees or fly
four ways or eat a bit of moth
but it was not or never,
it was not enough.

He shook the jar, he quaked it.
A punch for a dollar.
A thrust for a laugh.
He reached. Boy, he reached.
Rattled or shook,
so each disfigurement,
sampled in glass,
was simple and settled
and quiet, a carapace of dust.

Reclamation

Flies dart over the broad back of the corpse,
wrestling among hairs and crawling the stilled eyes.
They'd found it at the reservoir under partial light,
the unplumbable mire a clot of scum, splayed insects,
catkins from a near alder, an ochre float of willow leaves.
Their old dog hanging in telluric shallows.
Probably he'd lost his legs, straining til his heart gave out.
Maybe he'd gone on purpose with an unforgiving thirst.

Underwater the rust-red hairs swam ethereal
and fine as silk. Free, at last, of gravity.
His father hoisted the forelegs and he, the hind.
They brought the body to the air
where the water broke. The hind paws
cold and stiff as the knobby hilts of a wheelbarrow.

Now they smack stones with their spades,
upheel an ancient complication in clay.
Black flies, mosquitoes graze their ears, a mist
slender as a small death between the birch,
a surrounding sway of mute-white boughs.

The two men cut a stark space, attacking,
between the shovels, a lacrimal till.
Breaths were broken out. A matt
of root that met the pointed drive. The steep
assault of scent like brooding tea: a slant
of clubmoss, clouded pancreatic crawl
unbolted in the wane. Their dog,
a blanked, compromising slate.

His father rears up from the work
to daub his face. In the crooked light
he looks as if he's making strange signs,
like he did at the Rutland ball diamond,
signage the son was never sure of.
Both are backed with a shadowy
braid: it funnels from their feet,
a shrunken, whispery connivance of flies
that rakes apart the dog, a wasp
that scales the retracted tongue, the good teeth.

An after-breath in the gapped. A droning
reek, a drowning. The drill of muskeg
makes them tighten as they loosen
earth, a plot they scrutinize
between the planted spades—
aspen, fireweed, auricular in the dusk—
before they swing the carcass across the dark.

Under wet fractals of spruce-light
where robins sew for worms,
hued crackle of turf-leaf,
leaf-shadow, for which his father stops.

Leathering

He travels north from camp to camp,
trailers on dunnage, gravel,
rusted barrels and stacked wood,

tents where men dream cement,
its consistency, its price,
the length of its fix.

He forgets his reasons, his debts, his wife,
works a ditch or drives a spike.
There is a stone in his wrist.

He craves the cracked-up moon, the lake,
a place on the mud bank to shout, to drink,
to fuck under the stars.

He'd like a newer pouch, tools with clean
teeth, straight lines to gouge
geometry in peat, a level he can trust.

Mosquitoes have eaten his skin.
His thumb is black. Clouds
fatten through the west.

What lasts is law: that axis breaks
on axis, rain on rain.
If he could reach, he'd pull

every twisted star with a hammer.

Contact

In the digital flash of three a.m.
at the Best Western, he's awake,
the ceiling fan, the heat,
a fibreglass fuse on his skin.
While Lisa sleeps, both shoulders
covered, he realizes she's been crying,
lip gloss on her open mouth,
eyeshadow a dusted flutter of wings.
Inside her blouse, her breasts
heavy to his touch—they're numb,
both his hands to the wrists.

At eighteen he joined the infantry.
Near Wainwright, training,
it was forty below, they were firing shells,
he shed his gloves to fix the radio
and lost all feeling. In Afghanistan,
hills glutted with men triggering
rounds through the scrub,
his rifle fuming,
he forgot the local
smokes were primed with opium.

He's twenty now and works for his father
in the north end, every day in harness,
rising with a skyscraper, half-built.
He wanted tomorrow off. Yet
asking his father, he was queasy.
He couldn't face the old man, so instead
walked out. What kind of soldier,
son, he asks himself, runs?

His rage, his lust, is on the other side of his wrists.
The guy whose chin he smashed, yesterday
after work, was lumber under steel.
Women too were pictures he called up,
overlaid on websites, neon-cheap,
on the rig-pig in the tight shirt
whose glance swelled shut before the brawling quit.
He saw so many women, he liked
the honest ones, he figured
it was in their pose, the mouth of course—
through a filter weather in the eyes.

That's what he saw through the crowd,
through the sputtering shrapnel of the strobe,
Lisa under the speakers wearing a red
blouse with her left shoulder exposed,
sharp in his circuitry. He was charged
by the men standing close, everyone's
desire soldered to his own, the smooth
open fire of her dancing. He felt
her up at the bar. He was never
so bold before his hands went blind.
She didn't say much, even later,
his hands sweeping
her skin, his mouth on her body.

Through the balcony screen, the summer,
hard-going, carries on. If he were to sleep,
he might confront his father's
slipping gaze, years in a company hat,
hair matted, losing lustre. But,
who is sleeping, and who,
now, has been crying?

Ladybugs

He swats them as they graze his teeth.
A slow propulsive battery. They veer
toward his throat or pupil. Frieze
of pebbles. Float of hail. Disturbed
heat in susurration on the fifth floor.
Spitting out a third, he lifts the rail
from its u-ring perch and signals Sam,
the tar-black bastard forking panels
up or down on a boom. Opal blue.
Aspen. He pauses at the bright pillar,
its surfaces unctuous, unbroken, and cool.

Another ladybug beads him in the eye.
He stumbles. At the edge
the crew in hardhats, insect-small.
With a pivot, discrete, vaulted,
he snags the neat end of the nearest rail,
two-by-four pinched
between a gloved thumb and forefinger.
A too-large glove, its leather
too worked out in a sheen.
He fronts his weight. Yearning to
a distance shaded on the floor.
Oh fuck. Each word—his voice
is cleated—tapped home
like the head of a nail.
His harness, rope,
are buried on a hook in the sea-can below.

Such awfully ordinary laziness, that near fall.
His pulse freaking out. Yesterday a journeyman
Buddhist insisted a life may be measured by heartbeats—
an espresso addict, a centuried monk differing just
in the pace of the beat or length of breath. So
he follows a chalk-line of coke,
heartbeats clipping free like all those dotted ladies,
hundreds madly honing, horny,
spuming from trees to the pillar and his body
where the boom rises or falls as he waits at the edge.

Pulses, lugged through papery skin, discomfited him.
Not blood, but its arterial wheezing, repulsed him.
His father's death by cardiac arrest.
When would his heart attack—that bankrupt
glutted tempo lobbing every valve?
Cocaine stinted the heart, but it brought sharpness,
red wing, black wing, glazed with frost.

From Cabin Hill

Before the boomtime, they weren't capable of selling
  flyers or flipping
burgers, let alone roughing it on girders or the rigs.
Built wrong, they were arsonists, soothsayers, detox drifters.
Like Danny, who muttered to himself and drew on outhouse walls
his co-workers, whose faces were mashed through
by a hammer. When he caught me eyeing him
he made the devil's hand and flashed his large lesioned tongue.
I hauled a sixteen-footer from the grass, vexed with mosquitoes,
grunted as I jacked it vertically so he could reach. He swayed
on his end, leaden, blinking, fucked in the shop.
Of course the Boss ignored this, bought some tearjerk tale,
how as a single father, fending off an ex-wife in court,
Danny was burping a baby all night, every night.
It could have been true, he'd sleep at lunch face planted to the table.

Or the Acid Hippie, hair past his ears, who in the west corridor
installed drywall with a stereo so loud you heard the hissing
strings of Zeppelin, Floyd, or Hendrix through the duct
twenty-six stories down, when you cupped your ear to the grill.
His last job, in Newfoundland, he scalped as a carnie
for a migrant fair, until, the story goes, there was an unborn son.
Deaf to traffic, he slept in a small tent floored with pelts,
hemp fabric pegged by the highway, obscured in thickets.
His wristwatch showed the hour, not the minute. Often late,
he stayed late, climbed the chain-link after lock-up,
  ears still ringing.
He signed on with us, maybe, because we had electric outlets
and the Boss in a lapse didn't snip his stereo cord.
When we had the blackout for a week that winter, electricians

wiring the upper floors, I slouched upstairs for batteries.
He was gone. His gloves gripped a sheet of gypsum board
as if he were fried to an airy dust.

Then there was Fat Gunnar, Foreman of the Brickies,
who bullied other trades, tearing left or right
without safety goggles, hardhat, or a mask, inhaling
deeply that abraded shroud of silica.
Piled with cinder-blocks, his pallets teetered
at the end of scaffolds. His men
reached from the highest rung of ladders. Rifled
through lunches, pocketed drill-bits, boxes of screws.
Johnny Lightning warned us,
If you're gonna write him up, you better have balls—
he'll be ripping around with that goddamned cell-cam.
I yelled at Gunnar, he practically dared me,
bareheaded under a crew stripping a ceiling.
Spotted him after in front of the Boss, hardhat in place.
Lookie, I said, you found it. He roared, Who the hell're you?
General contractor, I said, staring. Nah, he spat,
You're just a fucking monkey! He busted me that afternoon
past the painted line without a harness.
Snapped eleven pictures, leveraged every angle.
But he got his. He'd ribbed a guy for days,
an older, lightweight Ethiopian
known for his workday hustle and few words.
You know what this is? Gunnar said, pinching a penny
under the guy's nose—An Ethiopian stranglehold!
That same punchy laugh. Then the old man
grabbed Gunnar by the neck and threw him to the ground.
Took four athletic brickies to pry those fingers from his throat.
The rest of the day, Gunnar mixed mortar in a daze.

Adam was a wannabe whitehat, cozying the Foreman, Lead Hand,
his beak so far up their asses we wouldn't know
who spoke if it weren't for his bright orange shirt and yellow stripes.
We called him Big Bird. Even that Bible-thumper
couldn't bear the roundabout way Adam spied
or his gab about work when all we wanted was quiet.
If we lingered, after lunch, he stood at the door,
clapped and rubbed his hands, faking the laid-back angle—
Ready to get at her?—underbitten lisp and flexed grin.
Bible-thumper dropped his paper—Are you signing
the cheques, boy?—and as Adam stamped off—
There ain't no better word for that kid than *princess*.
He talked and talked about his three-hundred-dollar hammer.
Johnny'd laugh—Now if you knew how to swing it.
He told the grossest stories, how he once hired a woman
for ten dollars, and she was so dry, he hawked a loogie
to lube the action. Another was so obsessed he feared
she'd scoop his sperm from used condoms and impregnate herself.
The more he tried to impress, the more we hated him.
Cutting trim as I passed, his rat eye swivelling,
he said, Damn it, then dropped a disposable blade to the concrete.
Running his knife toward himself he had slit
through his thumb, blood hopping from the artery.
He rushed away. I followed the splats
outside, where they diluted in the mud. In the First Aid room
he wrapped paper towel around his thumb
and pulled his shirt up over his head, pale as a worm.
We agreed, later, we'd never liked him better.

The Albanians, wary in the manner of brothers who are hunted,
crossed a cattlegate to the site, hoodies drawn, in wet July.

They were boys in Kosovo when their mother
was shot on the street. The eldest,
Kreshnik, was a trained cage fighter. Wore sunglasses,
was silent. I could never tell, when he piled
beams incorrectly or retrieved a chain we didn't need,
if he misunderstood, or if, in his cunning,
he meant to goad me. His brother,
Avni, would explain Kreshnik as we stripped
forms of a lower floor. He was the only one
unafraid of the Foreman, who, confused himself,
smiled when Avni asked, Why do they call you
Johnny Lightning? The Foreman turned away, then
spun around, fist and forearm clenched, Pow!
I am the flash before the thunder! He rolled his sleeve,
the sundered storm clouds a wrinkled tattoo beneath his shoulder,
and the young Albanian beaming. Later that summer
the brothers pinned the carpenter from Iraq in the basement. He'd
corrected their efforts too often, and now,
sent for u-heads on a pallet, they lowered his face
to the water, a foot in depth and mired with larvae. Avni
whispered in his ear, You don't give us orders, you dirty Iraqi,
and after making him beg, they let him go,
packed their gear and crossed the cattlegate one last time.

Tyrrel, or Tyrone, we were never sure which,
the Slavic engineer who oversaw oil refineries
before the Soviets withdrew from Georgia.
He took a shine to me, I can't say why,
I'm fair, maybe, I spoke up for him at break,
others chewing on how slow he was, how slothfully
he pulled nails from lumber, collected them like tokens.
Did anyone else, as I did, know how much metal he
hoarded in lidded buckets behind a stand of aspen,

severed ends of rod, angle-iron, slips of tin,
wrangled bundles of tie-wire?
Tyrrel had this habit of touching. As we met
to wind cord or pile sheets of fibreboard,
he'd ask what types of wine I liked, where did I go
for a dance, what did this city offer, resting
the upper portion of his hand on my elbow or waist
or draping his arm over my shoulder.
All I do is work, I told him, I don't know anything,
and reared back, nervous, scuffing my boot in the dirt.
The crew, dog-like, sunk its teeth variously.
Late that summer, his last shift, five of us carried posts,
shook out panels, set them to form,
shoring for the concrete pour on Monday.
We ran into a problem, arguing then
how we'd set the row over the guardrail.
Tyrrel stood in the midst of us, square jaw
floured with stubble, high cheeks lightly
tanned. Listening for a solution
they stopped, closed in.
Blue horses, he said, his English still imperfect,
when you call them in, they like apples. His thick lips
puckered, smacking, his hand extended,
he must have done this in the apple valley
with his brothers—we were staring—
his fingers brushing together—he stopped us
short—as if he were gauging
a fabric for his sister's dress
or rubbing the bracts of a grain, calling us,
horses, men, to the sweetness in his palm.

Drill / Screw

The weight's in the battery. Pass it on. Trade it for another when it's dead. Sometimes you blow on it or hit it up, wrap it with duct tape. But don't ask for help. If the cabinets need lifting or the hinges held in place, plant the jig and try it yourself. Turn the light on or turn it off. Perch on a bucket for the uppers. Fuss with screws, the long ones, the short ones. Stand them in the square bit and swear as they fall, tapping the concrete, tapping a hundred times.

You get a call from your boss. You stack plywood or stop a flood or carry a barrel. It's been a year since you wrenched the building out of mud. Now, the hours just the same, you plug deficiencies. You go back to what you were doing. Quit fucking the dog.

When the screw's balanced, between the bit and the board, you hope your wrist stays true and the angle's right. The hammer-drill is easier, but if you aren't careful, you might rip through the drywall, smooth as milk. You press the trigger and the glare of sound, the pushed hot shriek of it, tears the scab off your nerves. The screw strips, along the neck or at the head, or the cabinet goes out of level, or there's no backing, because some bastard didn't put it in, and the coil grips the air or insulation, nothing else. Maybe you get a bite two times out of ten. Maybe you don't.

Across the room, a wasp is all twisted up. He gathers his face and his parts where the glass slides. His stomach, his wings can't get him through. You hear the bones in your body, the granite in your voice. You feel the ache around your eyes, the ramming blood, the cracked retinas—the sixteenth hour, the forty-eighth, the sixty-eighth—forty-seven days without a break. Drywall dust whitens your hairs, the tips of your lashes, the bags in your chest. You work in the dark. You even dream of this, white drifts on the sill, the cleavage of your brain. Granular women in dresses of dust. There is a trace in the corridor, in the joint of the cord, heavy as a python. There is a pitch, like tossed flour, in every breath.

Johnny Lightning and the Safety Meeting

The subject of today's meeting is fall protection. Before you scale the roof, check your harness, inspect the stitches and webbing, the D-ring and the buckles. If you find any nicks, frays, or twists, we'll take it out of service. Check the lanyard and the lifeline too. When you're up there, scan the guardrail and the toeboards, make sure they're in place. Remember, falls are the second-highest cause of death in construction.

This issue's timely. In Calgary, some guy tripped over a ponywall, tied off to a piece of scrapmetal. Now, that scrapmetal caught, he was okay, but his harness, it wasn't snug—a strap was twisted near the groin—so his balls were blown out of his sac down his fuckin knee. As big as this coffee cup, after the swelling. And heads're gonna roll. That's why Safety's busting my ass.

Maybe you heard, me and Safety Sean got into a bit of a headbanger today. First thing off Monday morning, he asks, You have a few minutes? I say sure, so he rattles away. Your guys aren't wearing protective goggles. Your extension cords have frayed fuzzies around the plug or the casing's cracked over winter. One of the chopsaws has a screw fixed in the guard. And the trailer floors're unswept.

My first thought is, I'm gonna eat this cocksucker alive. Why don't he ever finish his audit and say, Everythin's good? I have more critical shit to do out there than listen to him bitch about the floors. But he's from Industrial. They have that million-dollar budget to keep someone cooked on bullshit like that. I said, If dirty floors is in the report, I won't sign it, and he said, I don't need your signature. Well, if he writes me up, I'm gonna throw the bastard one helluva curveball.

Don't be fuckin owly, the Boss says to me, after what happened in Calgary, Safety's under pressure. All right, but there's a special place in hell for a guy who never gets his shirt dirty, and I'm gonna tear him a new ass. The reason I became a carpenter was I wanted to build things. I like getting the guys ready, gearing em up in the mornings. Instead, I'm filling forms, like those zombies at head office. I'm being dragged all over site by a fuckin muttonchop.

Now, keep this under your hats, it's the same with the LEED program. They want an eighty-five percent redux in material sent to the landfill. Okay, but the measuring system's whacked. If you have carpenters who measure proper, a Project Coordinator who orders the right amount of material, you're penalized. We're given points for waste sent to recycling, measured by weight, no points for good planning. We've seven massive bins we don't have room for, bins for debris, drywall, metal, cardboard, concrete, plastic, and wood. When I told the LEED Inspector, I could pour cement straight into the bin, come out on top, he said, Yeah, I guess you could.

Construction ain't fun anymore. You can't put girls in bikinis on the wall, because some uptight bitch might peek through the fence, but they're fit to publish at the back of the city paper? That don't make sense. What if it's a picture of my wife? Now we have that fucking otter smiling at us from the calendar. I could see if it's a distraction—hell, then you might as well ban women from the streets. Boys, remember this, if you're eleven stories high and your mind's on the sidewalk, you'll end up face-down in the morgue. Fact is, I don't allow catcalls, you all know that, yet for all intensive purposes, sexual harassment is the only crime in this country where you're guilty until proven innocent. Ten years ago I was renovatin a school when a kid tells his teach I wanna bang her. I got suspended without pay for four days, and after being cleared, I was transferred. Fuck that. Anyhow, enough said. Get back to work.

The Cleaning Girl

The vacuum's suck and crackle
drew his ear across the dingy corridor.
He carried a tray of paint, a fresh
brush for a touch-up on the door-frame.

"Hey-o," he said, knuckle at the pine.
"Careful of the frame, eh?"
She nodded. Glanced,
noted his mud-caked tread.

·

Sometimes his face was just a routine
tremor solidly held, his eye's
twitch a sign he was nervous,
closed in with weariness.

Broom aslant on his shoulder he entered
uncarpeted corridors loud and echoey
with a welder's torch, the shunt of a drill's
give-out and the requisite swearing.

"How's she going?" the Foreman pressed.
"Round and round," he said.
The stairwell wavered like a watery pool,
reflective, underlit by a distant bulb.

·

At second coffee he laughed with the rest
as the Pentecostal Cape Bretoner
weighed in on Fort Mac, "City's
full of Lego ladies, man.

Fake hair, fake lip, from head to toe.
You wake with a snapper, all right. A face
so rough you could hang your coat on it.
Not some smoke-show like your girl."

They traded doubtful tales of this or that girl,
harelipped settled-fors or trophied
encounters with a boss's daughter. What
mattered was polish. Sweep in the telling.

•

They went quiet when she walked by,
dressed, not in the usual pastel
uniform, but in street clothes—
above the neckline, milk-pink, hale,

a trailing daub of perfume—trim
belt about the ribs—a jacket
neatly awning her waist,
discreet, impervious to the bait.

"Have a nice night," he said,
overlapped by the Cape Bretoner.
"You too," she said, cleaner
than winter, toward the parkade.

Soon, the back-and-forth of who it was
she said words to. Reluctant
and all knots, they weren't equipped
to know or say, how noiselessly

a small frost had entered her, something
lethal, unmanicured. So they circled,
interpreters of fractional contact,
clipped their belts and went back to it.

Winter Night

Inside the half-built tower after shift the heaters thrum and fan
within the hoarded corridors, outer walls, stairwells,
hemorrhaging where he stares—the orange tarp winging
reflexively the unpaned window of the fourth floor—
the boiler room with its boxed units, gypsum rock sheeting
the studded perimeter, a coat of white paint wafting—
he watches shadows from the hall splay across cement
and snubs his cigarette in a sack of hardware at his feet,
the foreman's interfering din far off. The work this season's
mostly custodial—sweeping, tracking halogens for the bricklayers,
carting debris in wheelbarrows, pumping vats of water
leaked in from the fluted q-deck, drilling holes, hasping doors,
and banding pallets for the boomlift. The night's a twelve-hour
life tacked to the board with every loopy, underfunded sleep.

The broom's a milky blot, the jack of faucets, even his ashen boots,
all a slurring cargo through his eyes, a gravid focus
forewarning the ruff of pain in half an hour—if his truck's
cache of pills is gone, which he fears it is—his head
        as wide as the street,
wadded with soot and snow, every melt of light an optic
clutching that leaves him curled in any shuttered closet he finds,
good for nothing the rest of the restless night. But that's
        in half an hour.

Now he starts another cigarette—the probing blood behind his eyes
reminds him of the lake in Creston, paved with ice,
that winter he was canned from the welding crew, his urge to yell
lofted like the spray from a stricken rooster's neck—

the air's chilled slide winnowing the smoke, his thoughts,
beyond the rectangular fray, himself even sliding through,
    tractioned,
the aspen leaves glassily blanched, the tower itself crystalled
where rain collided yesterday with plastic and the steel—
stars meanwhile teeming the two o'clock scrim, the prospering
convolutions of cloud, yes, the excruciated aging stars.

The Bug Unit

They hired Sean after he was with us a week
through the local Bug Unit, a rent-a-labour
outfit of ex-cons, addicts, welfare yahoos.
Nice guy and all, he was clean,
he was Cree from out east. Had attention
deficit, had it bad. Like,
he'd fly at hard work, strippin ply.
All one speed, Go, go, go. Faster
than a squirrel in a barn chase
but fuckin reckless
for what needed smarts or a sober look.
The Boss knew it and he tried
to put him where he was best at, smashing rocks,
gatherin garbage, movin crates.
When he was thrown with us
strippin scaffold, he took lead.
Me and Dane were at wide berth. That's
no place for him: above us
on a platform banging at what was
always a death trap, really, panels, beams,
ready to swing at a sneeze. Well,
Sean gets impatient when he can't loosen
the post-crown with a tap
so he kicks the post like a mule,
the whole ceilin rainin down.
We come out dancin but he was half-purple
where a panel had cracked his head.
Kept working though, I'll give him that,
shredding air guitar and howling the blues:
"Cuz I'm blue," he said, pointing to the bruise.

When there's an Indian on site
there's always guys'll say, He's good
for an Indian. But he was good.
If I had trouble loosenin them clamps
he was quick to share the trick,
he didn't lord it over no one.
He'd microwave a slab of smoked salmon
plastic-wrapped on styrofoam
and hold it out. "Have a bite,"
he'd say. "It's the cat's ass, man." But that
always put me off, more than melted plastic.
He'd make us laugh. "I was so poor,"
he'd start. "Hotdogs on Monday. Weiner
soup on Tuesday. By Wednesday
I had to jerk off the dog to feed the cat."
Or he'd grin, "You got Indian blood?"
No, I'd say. "You want some?
Bend over. I'll pay you out a bit
of my Indian bone marrow."

His old lady had her shit together.
Owned a car, a house near site.
They were both stoners, but he was
getting worse: it calmed his fidgets, he said.
He was smoking a spliff one night
burning through their stash, her basement
vents sealed shut with poly: she
raked him over, threatenin
to throw him to the curb—what does he do?—
takes his paycheque for a three-day bender,
smokes sixteen hundred in crack.

When I seen him next Sean's at my door
high as a kite with a blown-out lip,

a burst vessel shot through the white
of an eye, his limbs all stutter.
He was a hundred pounds lighter
but then he only weighed a hundred to begin with.
He'd come hunting for cash, a couch.
I gave him a hundred bucks.
Last I'd see of that, I knew.
I couldn't help but watch as he ate.
Literally he sobered. Thawed.
One eye open. One eye shut.
Tipped over asleep. You
could've taken a shit on his face,
he wouldna known it till mornin.
That third night, I said,
You can't come here no more, Sean.
Not like this. Talk to your wife.

He missed work. Lost his job. The talk
was that he was no exception, right,
he was what we knew him from the start.
Jay don't give him a dime that night Sean
trespass on site: so his truck
was sprayed in bright orange,
Jay liks the cock. The cops were called.

We were sure it was him who flocked
a bag of syringes in the drywall bin,
and him who peppered the toilet lid,
that roll of shit-tickets, with bear mace,
and me whose asshole was quiverin
first with a burn, like a fist
of jalapenos up my bunghole.

Last I seen him I'm drivin in town.
This dumbass to my right, bone-thin

in a white hoodie, he shoulder-checks
real fast to cut out across but he don't see.
I pound the brakes, his head side up
to the bumper. Could've been a smear
of bug guts on the windshield. I shout,
Hey, Limp-Dick, What're you doin?
When buddy turns, it's Sean, snarlin,
"Don't you mean-mug me, you prick."
It's like he don't recognize me at all.

Storm

In groups of three, you pin the column forms, push every minute for the next pour. Keep on it, Larsen shouts. The trucks don't stop and neither do you. Rain starts lashing in, the blackness flashes. In the tie of the pour, the impossible schedule, no one sleeps, least of all the Foreman. Goddamnit! Half-braced, one of the forms, the eastward length of the elevator shaft, lifts in the wind. MacLean yells and the others run, the downbeat belly of the fall, the hammers, the six-inch nails. You're careful not to slip, eight ladders to the mud.

For an hour, in the lunch trailer, MacLean's white. His teeth itch, he says. Still, he slugs his coffee with the rest. The youngest, Adam, brags through a story from Fort Mac, how a girl, when he ran out of cash, fucked him anyway, in the cold rear-bed of a pickup. Dinging the light, moths hover. He's nervous and so are you. Two flies ruminate the lunchbags under the table, stitching eggs in scraps of meat. You turn the pages of a porn mag. Though you like the mouths, the moths, they seem to be blowing in your ear, you don't feel right.

Outside the sun is gone and there is only blackness, a fog of black. The aspens plunge, right from left, the ash-white aspens in the wind. You hop from stones to a plank, crossing ruts of earth, to the office. Like the lunch trailer, it floats on dunnage, slags of concrete. You knock on the perforated plate of the window. Someone calls you in.

His desk piled with extension cords, a drill that smokes and sparks, you pass the Foreman. He stops you with the slow wearing in his jaw, the bad connection in his head, the cord he's prying apart. *Eh?* His grip loosens on the pliers. Behind the door, open just a crack, the Boss is talking in a low boil. Among the boots and pails there is a candle. A giant pike held by a jag of wire in the Boss's fist. Through the wound at its throat, the creature is bubbling. The Boss props the fish on the wall, where it bleeds, and the candle, which falters into smoke, is blown out. Outside, the blackness thickens.

Entertainments

Five o'clock Friday the men stowed their gear in the lunch trailer, tugged free their boots and tossed hardhats on hooks. Outside the wind gripped the walls, vice-like, the metal whistling. Skiffs of rain stiffened and speared, the hail slapping hard. Brad poured himself a drink from the cooler using an empty soup can for a cup. You'll cut yourself, said Sam, leaning back. Nah, said Brad, wiping his stache, I've kissed women with sharper tongues than this. Someone laughed, Sure you have, and Iain grinned, Yeah, those weren't women, those were deer.

Sometimes birdsong boiled at them outside, noises like eggs weaving in a pot, surging to that click of shell. They were themselves tires under so much dirt, coils from a mattress worn to the frame. Keezer looked out the window, and he did not say, as he might have wanted, that he saw from the ricocheted limbs of aspen, fabric filling out like sails, ragged billowing dresses. There was so much none of them could say as the gabble boiled to steam.

To forget the weather, Keezer stared at Brad. Quit it, Brad said. With an unwavering blankness, Keezer recited a poem, and it wasn't that good, but good enough, it rhymed. By the fourth verse, the guys laughed. The Foreman, with a slavering cough, entered the trailer. Stopped at Keezer's side, staring.

By Keezer's ninth verse, the Foreman interrupted with a tobacco-y spit, shifted foot to foot before dragging from his cigarette. You slag! he sang, You bag, you slippery slimy slut—fungus grows between your toes and crabs crawl up your cunt. Before I lick those scabby legs and suck those withered tits, I'd drink a litre of buzzard juice and die of the drizzlin shits. See. You're not the only one who can talk.

Iain covered his eyes. Sam laughed into the table. Conrad, flagging Keezer, asked him, How'd you do it? He reads, Iain said, his lip curled. The Foreman coughed again. Yeah, that's what happens when you read. I was sittin in a shitter in Saskatoon when I saw it written on the wall.

The wind screamed under the kickplate of the door. How'd you do it? Conrad asked again. Keezer toyed with a wrapper from a Kit Kat bar, ripping it in half. I guess I wrote it at the hospital after listenin to Leonard Cohen. Conrad tied his shoes. What, the guy from *Star Trek*?

When the crew had gone, the Foreman clapped Keezer on the shoulder. Don't take much to entertain em, does it? He scratched his jaw. What they don't know is our beards make us actors. Piss poor, maybe. But if we didn't have em we'd be little pussies like the rest. The Foreman slung his toolbelt on a hook as a car sped onto the street. Before he stepped outside, he asked, You okay? Keezer nodded. All right. The Foreman tapped the door. Lock up, will you.

The Boss

The Boss stowed clout and commendation—
this molten rush before the winter ice
an excavation wrought with trenching,
augercast piles topped with concrete, hurried
rebar cages the width of a waist
impelled through future slabs,
braided with wire, bar, a length of human hair,
an upright phalanx of columns the Boss
inspected with an engineer, whose integrity,
a frail green sprout, was corruptible in the field.
The tower's first phase completed a month early
at a fraction of the cost. So fast, his workers
traded rumours. On his walkabouts,
they said, he diffused from flesh
into fog, with only the heel-weight of his pace
forewarning his approach at the sleeve
of a rookie electrician or a squirmy apprentice.
However much the praise of peers or top brass, the Boss
spurred the crew and trades for more or less.
He consulted with an emptiness, the seepage
god beneath the barred concrete, the god of abscess,
not the Cross, not the many-tinted god of leaves or frost,
but the accrued god of javelins, oil slicks, mirrors,
microchips, the buzz or flash in thought
or culture, the wasting touch of light. He lost weight.
Sleep. Sent agents for smudge, twine,
locked himself at his desk or sealed himself
at the tower's bald upper reach.

Men opted double shifts for meagre pay,
every cord of muscle or unit of sweat a tithe to the Boss
who promised gifts or changed their minds behind a door.
Brickies lorded the necessity of brick. Sparkies, the necessity
of wire. Roddies disputed with bar and Plumbers with pipe.
Framers with stud. Finishers with board or plaster.
Roofers a brush of pitch. Welders the seething molten point.
It was the Boss himself who saw that each hooked in with each,
squarings, rivets, parapets, the tower extruding from the ground.

He wanted more. Harried his Foreman, who said,
We're running on fumes! Roddies, Brickies, they're on my ass!
Corked like a knotted thigh. The ravenous reave and grind,
machinery, supplies, subtrades, rib to rib with action, trash,
the quicker they huffed or heaved the slower it went.

They could not order diesel soon enough. They could not crane
angle-iron to the seventh floor or plywood or basins of water,
or patch an electric grid for the upper fringe, soon enough,
or wheel garbage to the bin—triangular cuts of the tinbasher,
a brickmason's gurney of slop, hair-thin copper bits under switches
and outlets, the pipe-fitter's tubular threaded scrap—none of it
cleared away soon enough but steeped in crannies and corridors
until the work stalled and every trade jawed for space.

The Boss rankled. Sizzled over his two-way radio.
Desk heaped with manuals, dispatches from HO,
sheets of graph pencilled with arcane arithmetic.
He trawled risks, taprooted eerily accurate judgment,
didn't balk at the stopped labour.

In the days ahead the tower climbed three stories. Tentative,
delayed with rumination, the Boss
read transmissions in the smoke, foundering indicators.
Uninformed, his Foreman crowed. Hung up his plastic slicker.
Clapped at the bulwark of cloud, its half-
imagined wagers of light. But that
burden rumbled for the worse. Spear-
headed rain that drummed without end. Slippages
so deep men lost footing, boots were shucked away,
machinery lurched in ruts a man could drown in.
Sleet-frosted layers of cotton or denim,
numbing skin, men couldn't keep a grasp on tools.
The Boss circled. As hailstones racketed hardhats
he shamed his youngest men by taking up their shovels, trowels.
Then as soon, a raking wind,
lightning fires crackling through trees right to the suburbs.
Houses were evacuated. Someone cut
hydraulic cables in the skidsteer and tapped the tread with nails,
litred the jerry cans with piss and bashed the lights on every floor.
Dust blew in, gritting the eye and everyone's spit.
Finally, the building flooded, every man rushing as water burst
the window panes to the ninth story, sluicing volumes.
It was then the Boss tossed his hardhat to the air—
scooping the sun from the sky as it passed—flooding them
    all in the black.

Mythologies of Men

Travis ate his carrots. Shaved at three. He built a motorbike from scrap, he built a stair-rail ramp, he built a fire. He mastered concrete finishing at five, he grew a fine goatee. His work-a-day pals, swift in that grey North Edmonton slum—stripped with plastic, neon-lettered shops, tulips made of wood, evenly potted saplings with steel-wire fetters— put a lot by him, for he wore a clotted eye like a badge. He loaned out cash, he loaned a truck, he loaned out strength, too often.

Though he didn't earn it, something in him faulted, a clinkered root, infected follicle of luck. First, his pencils, when he wrote at tests, trembled like a psychic's, fraught like the needle of a seismograph. Then came migraines, a sympathetic gift from dad, his granddad, swarming and paling. Then came nosebleeds. You could fill mason jars, crates, fill a sump or water main, the blood that sampled out of him. Travis had it bad. And in which ways did he fail, this fail-safe son, screw-up and scrapper, injuring himself? I say he dropped on the road like a ladled throw of water, beaded and brown in the dry lime. Launched from the seat of a skidsteer, he landed on a mud clump and tore the alert fastenings of his ankle. Toting strips of cedar trim, tacky from the painter's bench and bundled to a lift's inclined forks, he sucked a breath between his teeth, he caught a finger at the pinch where one strip smacked another, blood rallying at the nail, a bleat, a bleat, so it blackened and bucked. Moneymart took its tithe on him, sequestered cheques for the lien on him, for the truck, and the bike, and the quad, for the wrecking lot coke, the Jeet Kune Do, for the second truck, totalled in a dyke, or a third his brother burned with the lit end of a lazy roach.

The Super with his father's stache, a pair of prickly eagle wings, pointed to the ill-set concrete. Travis tamed it with a vibrator, screeded the swells, smoothed and stamped it with bull-floats, edgers, groovers.

The Foreman with his granddad's craven jaw pointed to an excavation. Travis, in a backhoe, cratered it with a bucket, jigged his treads against a slope of forty-five, undecided in those lightheaded teeter-totter seconds. The Super with Time's dry scalp pointed at the crawl space, where Travis stooped with weighted pails, ferried concrete to the roof, hurrying on his knees through hot and unclean air. The Foreman with God's louring, tractored eyes pointed to the tarmac. Travis disbanded in a scrawl of sweat that, briefly, gripped the pavement. The Super shouted, You will be stung by a surgical wasp. Avalanched by an aerosol drop. Given a flange of death in a blood cell.

Travis thumbed a strip of skin discoloured and slivery with shoulder-hefted batts, insulations knit with fibreglass that brushed his neck and wrists the day he stacked bales of it by the trailer-load at the bay, a team of mulish boys on high and another dragging from the skidsteer's forked pallet the loosely wrapped bundles, light burdens to begin that ended in wide trawlings of breath, distended backs, and a persistent long-hand itch. Slack on a stool at the Kicking Horse, he drank a fifth Molson, became philosophic and agape when a keno addict with flaxen hair spread his frayed blue-jeans, foraged his mouth with a violent tongue before she circled his chair and reached into his pocket, his right not his left, a stroke of luck. She slurred away with twenty, not three hundred dollars.

Repairing an apartment balcony he tumbled when the plywood flaked, his one good foot impacted, shut and pulverized. Pronged in the bank, a rod of rebar he slipped through that nicked his aorta, ruptured his neck, essential fluids, airs, commingling at the new passage, blouting at the swale, the drainage. There was more of his blood out in the world than had ever been in him. This disgorgement, suffering's pyroclast, carried on flooding: across acreages, roadways through the Rockies, it slid through tarsands, marshes and lakes: his blood averted into dust wherever it passed among the prairies, his bones so cracked with heat

their powders became a seminal itch among the spindles of idiotic pi-
geons or mice, his quintessence an improving talc or molasses: even
his smallest knuckle became a plug above a log fire, his length of femur
a tongue-suck in a weasel's hole, his fig-mishapen ear a saint's relic at
the Fort Mac Revival, rope of texture in the rapeseed soup: his bits and
fibres scoring all who ate or wore them with unaccountable strengths,
until powder's powder split in the dirt, an agitation, and kinnikinnick
grew there, and sage. A seizured, embryonic kindling.

Johnny Lightning and the Apprentice

In the upswerve slog of morning Johnny waged
over the soil, marking slab-grades with a stake,
its electronic beep measuring the slope's highs, lows,
between the toolbelt's toss and clank.
Cocksucker, cried Johnny, stake flying,
That queer picks his
calculations from the compacted
cul-de-sac of his ass! And I oughta know,
I've done everything from gas to glycol, goddamnit,
balls of wax—that bastard's more
slippery than a shit-caked cantilever!

Unfastening his collar, he smacked his lap, denim
gristed with caulking. Spat to the dirt,
and spotted me loafing on a barrel my first shift.
His coarse hands a set of pincers clasping mine
he frothed at the air, finger-thin ponytail
whipping like a stiff skip-rope round and round.
I was no good—a college kid like that scrawny engineer
revising blueprints, elevations, in blurred pencil—
another part-time worm who shovelled shit
uphill or tripped in two-inch holes.

Yeah, I was a rook, tender-footed, an aproned
pussy with a clean shirt,
supple academic hands, but I bled.
After five years tied up at the tower
my tongue was frayed but free,
under Johnny, Foreman of the crew,
under his Boss too.

Eight of us split a condo, company-owned. Squatted.
Three were Newfoundlanders. Two from Ecuador.
All of us company carpenters, here from away,
drudging a life on Friday nights, Sundays, paydays.
Someone's ex dumped us and ditched her dog—
we kept it—a Pomeranian that snarled from its cage.
Bared its teeth when Johnny shook a tin of treats
or jangled a leash or puffed or whistled. The biter,
blind, had infected, milk-jellied eyes—
no matter how madly Johnny doused the animal with water
it snapped and spun after its tail, leaking vomit on its towel.

Each morning he drove me to the site, he blared the radio,
cursed on the horn if some prima donna didn't gear
at the green or tailgated if a Chink braked at the merge.
After shift, when my head dipped groggily, he'd swerve
his truck to the ditch shouting Dear Jesus
or belt me in the arm with a pipe he kept under his seat.
Stopped in traffic he bullied pedestrians,
Put some panties on girl, you'll cause an accident! Or,
loudly with the window down, That girl had
       crescent-wrench eyes.
Christ, she looked at me and my nuts got tight!
Or at Big Iain's wedding: Johnny's cell-phone
with every digital click zoomed in on some girl's tits
as tailored guests, neatly seated, crossed their arms.

iv.

In the kitchen after midnight, Johnny'd play poker online.
Basted in sweat on summer nights, I drank
the cold swill thickening in the coffee pot
where he'd wire up gambling next to the sink.
He tried to sell me goose shit. Like how Nibiru,
Planet X, is set to swing through the solar system,
throw Earth's axis out and ignite a glut of storms
nipping ninety percent of this ragged-ass race to the bone.
But, he said, you'll survive if you've a trade
or a tattoo in Egyptian. Planet X.
Stargate for the Sumerian shape-shifters, spanglers,
lizards caked in human meat among twin-
tongued Senators and Presidents, spacious tanks of piss,
rigging the jig. Look, he said,
pointing through glass to a pink cluster in space.

Johnny never shared his apocalyptic tales
with anyone but me, nor his fondness
for the roses congealed against the wall,
the bollard-line tug of alcohol,
nor the predictable narrative of ex-wives
he savoured like marbled fat on a steak.

v.

When head office offered me six months in Fort Mac
Johnny huffed. Oh you don't want that, he said,
highballing coke-tweaked addicts and every slut
lubricating her cunt with your paycheque. Hell,
when they forced me north on a two-year turn,

trades crowing their fat mouths, the local Super
cooped in his trailer—I didn't know if I'd cry or strangle them all—
I was cankered when they sent me home.
The Boss was pissed. He's the Toy Maker,
you know, Calibrator for the Broken Toys—
they undid years of his work, flipping me north.
They'll give you a turn of the screw too, if you let em.

vi.

The project slumped, a spiring wreck of thirty-seven stories.
Johnny let me alone. Trusted I could run
what was on the go and in fair time. But, God. Flouted
through the heat, splattershod, I was at the end of it,
grime weathering my bandages four years in the job.
Seasons sludged. We sprayed the deck,
first with air to swat the stones and dust, then with oils
so the panels would pry free from the concrete
when it dried after the pour.
At the far end of the deck Johnny choked over a new hire—
he cinched on that boy's fear, brackish, a whiplash—
There's no man alive I'm afraid of, he said,
gathering spit from the back of his throat.

vii.

Long after the tower ended, we paired together on this or that.
I figured he got old when he slept in. He punted
around before dawn usually, but one time he
gaped at the stair railing. I'm sore all over—he swayed
drowsily at the knees—stuck in my joints like a tool left in the rain.
That summer we cribbed a bridge and built
retaining walls for school portables—clamped whalers, strongbacks,

nailed the kickers, sleepers—the tower still a bristling
palsy we'd never freed from the nerve. Even mucus
we expelled was flecked with debris.
Johnny's beard gone limpidly white, a scouring flurry.

I was outside the Peace camping with my girl
when the ringer on the cell sprung us from the fleece,
the canvas tent. Johnny raving at the roofers—
riddling obscenities from the ground—Move your shit!—
as they waved their fists, whistling, fingering him.
If you bastards think you're man enough, step up. Johnny
strutted gauntly, they said, even when he scaled the ladder,
inspected shingles, teetering pallets of garbage, tie-offs,
chucked another jibe, another, until the youngest roofer
batted his shovel-spade to the back of Johnny's skull.
He dropped. Twitched on the shingles, the grit,
spooling saliva for the length of an orange traffic light.

                    viii.

It's tough. You're on a leash for the cash when you get it,
collar of dirt at your neck. Some years the Boss
assigns the night shift, your thermos black or milted
with coffee-mate, the expired bulb of three a.m.
Sparks from the grinder cutting rod. The syncopated
drum of hammers, the deep-seated slam of the sledge.
Some nights I dream it was me on the roof, wild—
flesh beneath my thumb blistered with the grip or swing
of the shovel—tensed with half a century stripped bare
of weekends, litres of gas, insurance—just interest
on interest owed. Johnny's there
when I follow that aging crew to the tower,
sweating under the drill-bit stars, signalling
cranes and trucks with their bins of white clay.

The higher-ups will say the company records who
fucked off, who stayed, but when the spigot's dry,
they don't remember your name. That's what
Johnny said—Shit, you bank time, sponge,
tussle north or south, eat crow,
take a trowelled gob of lime in the face, expect
a jump-up or a raise?—Hell, all it ever got me was laid off!

Effluvia

The Archangel Michael, unearthly sword upright, spanned an entire wall with his wings, drawn in black pen. Lucifer, defaced, fanged, gloated over a stack of Sparkies, beheaded. Each outhouse was marked, the adversarial iconographers angering the Boss, who figured they weren't busy enough. Some guessed the Angel was Bill, a Pentecostal Cape Bretoner, while the meth addict Danny was Satan, announcing the End of Days. Both made a show of collapsing in the dust, gurgling the supreme tongue, whatever it was. In intervening spaces or across the clashing icons, men wrote limericks, phallic length, depicted *Gary's GF* with hairy tits, hyperbolic women tagged with telephone numbers, or hasty jibes, *The Boss fucks little kids.*

Whatever the graffiti, it distracted from the fusty odour, the absorbent dirt at the feet, the urinal with its dribblings of snot and sperm, the squatter everyone avoided. Talk at the lunch room ramped up when Big Iain proudly claimed a six-coiler at the peak of the mound, when Travis reported reams of tissue, sopped with blood, sign of some unanswerable tragicomic wound. To avoid that enamelled lid, some went as far as hovering, caking the seat when they missed. This pitched the Boss with such paroxysm he ordered locks on the outhouses for a month. Foremen, trusted with keys, were radioed whenever anyone needed in. To get even, someone left pails of piss in the boiler room.

When the wind battered through, a carpenter handling plywood nearly sailed off the cantilevered deck. Others heard nails squeal free as battened boards, buckets, flung over the side. Hardhats flew, spinning. Ladders toppled. When one of the outhouses lurched, tipped, there were whoopings and curses, but everyone mustered, careful, the rills of shit sloughing where the soil declined. As they prised the cubicle

with crowbars, pushed it erect, they heard shouting. *Shit, Adam's inside.*
Bootlicker, informant, he quickly tramped out—pulped from head
to toe in a fibrous slurry—woozily veering to the office. When it was
hot, weeks later, flies crowded the miasmal slop outside the outhouse
walls, dismantled it, until it was a blear, until it was less than a shade.

Dreamtime

He flew — yes, really. He jumped from the unfinished parapets and flew, his hammer a weight he'd cut free of, shooting off like a helium balloon some kid let go, and then, like an arrow, scutting out of line, the construction site a clearing in the forest. For a moment, he wheeled in space, like an idea, dove head-first to the aspens, leaf edges sharpening his sight, and it was like angels, it was like a party, the raindrops a parachute or a cape, his hands grazing the leaves, the leaves tickling his palms, lift, lift, with the changing weather. On the veined cuticles he could smell diesel floating over from the skidsteer, dust the raindrops kindled as they hit, and the cooling heated temperature of a damn good pour coming on.

His brother says take the stairs, so he does. His dead brother, but that doesn't faze him. In the dark, he opens the steel door, turns onto the landing, and every time, its floor slithers away and he flops into the lull, speeding to the south side of the building so he can boom a cart of scaffolds. A green and yellow can of corn bounces up out of a trench and strikes him in the face. His driver's seat is a chair in the trailer and he's eating from that cold can three times a day. Then he's counting cabinets through four hundred rooms and the numbers blur on his sheet at the prod of a pencil, he has to count them again, what was he counting? Hinges? Glides? Knobs? He's under a sheet of poly in one of the rooms, a painter's brush and the paint walloping the plastic over his chest. Then he stirs in the elevator shaft, plummeting. He stirs, face under plastic, his body rigid from the free-fall.

With his earbuds jacked in he listens to the iPod. To keep from getting caught in the closet asleep he suspends a pair of pliers that will jar him when they fall. If he wears earplugs instead, he hears a great volume of space caving at either direction, parentheses or corridors pointing to the scent of vanilla, to the cleaning girl who vacuums furnished suites. When he found her sweater yesterday in the north wing he brought it to his nose and inhaled. He last felt like that when he unplugged a water pump in the rain, the hum of it through his limbs. Clogged with perfume, he felt his neck and groin prickle, as they are doing now. He kisses her little wrists in the darkness, wrists he'd like to bite and taste marmalade. In her floral uniform, then her sweater, then undressed, she eases him to the ground, now a bed. Pears are tumbling out of her shirt, which becomes a gown, high-ridden. Together they swim, they sweat, along the corridor to the basement. She rocks violently over him, thighs like oiled fur, the curled ends of her hair brushing his chest. Sometimes she has charred stumps extending from her shoulders or she glistens not with sweat but an arid nakedness. Then he sees she is not human at all, but first a river otter, carrying the river and fetid with fish, and then a silver bear with sick sad eyes. Now she is human, and from the taut line of her body, smoother than concrete, he meets the unguarded tremors of her face. As he comes clumsily, she tells him, It's okay. She says, Sleep.

Rote Welter

i.

Chipping a massive disc of concrete in a bin. He couldn't remember
why. Maybe the city had rejected it, but he'd been at this work longer
than there'd been cities. He bullied the Hilti, the chickenhammer as
the Foreman liked to say, drubbing holes that might fracture thinner
parts. Sweat dripped from his hardhat. When the bit sunk too far and
it got stuck, he swore, tugging at the Hilti until his back ached, grease
scalding his hand. He took a chisel from his pouch, and a hammer,
and pounded around, hoping to get it free. When the chisel became
a stub, he applied the hammer's teeth, and then its ball, until the tip
came clear off. His fingers were okay for a while, but they got very little
done, his blood joining the sweat in the powdered concrete. This was
his work, his father's work. Entire tribes were assigned to it. He could
hear men toiling, approaching that long promise of rest. He didn't
raise his head to watch what they were doing, he didn't want to see.
He was observant like that.

ii.

In a rubber pail, he stirred the binder in water with a trowel, flattening
lumps in the blend. On his knees in the basement he poured the grout
between baseplates—where the beams ended—and the pile-heads
beneath. The runny mix was fixed on three sides with a form built
of two-by-fours, and on the fourth with a facing of hardened grout.
While he waited for this to firm, he moved back to another, tapped
its form with his hammer, and began to shave excess with his trowel,
trimming it flush with the baseplate, spitting on the trowel blade to
give the face a smooth finish. A cry echoed from the stairwell, trun-
cated by silence. He hadn't seen anyone since, well, he couldn't recall,

spring maybe, an electrician. He rinsed as much of the powder from his hands as he could. Once wet, it ate the skin. Already he was raw to the elbow, and it began to burn further, under his sleeve. When he was done one column, he moved to the next, and that was when he heard it, near the door to the stairs, a box being dragged, or a roll of poly. Outside his circumference of light, something he couldn't make out. He stood, reached for the silver bulb, and cast it on the creature, a three-headed buck, its coat glintless, its hooves soundless bells. One head nibbled at the throat of the body it had been pulling, a guy from Mechanical in coveralls. The second dipped a tongue into the blood. The last, snout to the floor, ears sprigged, looked up to stare at him inside his cage of light.

Demolition

He peers from beneath the lamp's white glare,
this scrubbed stranger's day-to-day
no different than his regulated beat
flogging composites. Mud, slate, cement.

The blank shine of dental hooks, surgical ends.

With scalers, curettes,
the gloved hand frets the sulcus,
batting dentin, clearing plaque. The gum's trough.

The dentist sticks the gum to dull
the nerve. An ill-defined
press of procaine twinges the ligament.

Wavering in view, an assistant's figure
and her neat laying out of tools.

Under a rotary drill, its air-compressed effort
fanning blurrily against his drugged cheek,
a chipped incisor, three black molars,
a fourth like split wood
spanning an open ache in the jaw.
Gums marred with drained blisters.

The drill-bit shrieks and spins. He hears the tooth's erasure.
The assistant's dogging-after with a sucking hose.
Crown-wheel, bearings, burs,
they flounder with the motor in a notch,
until, with an easy slide, they don't.
Churn, snag. The handler's corrected angle.

He knows that angle, knocking short
columns badly poured,
hammering concrete with a jack.

The grind of spackle, powdered enamel,
striving to his nose, and then,
the homecoming of pain under the drill.
More drugs. The dentist's dispassionate pause.

He glances in a dime-sized mirror
the half-way job, the wasted root.

Rubber-stubbed fingers shuck and score
the rinsed peneplain of bone.

Immobile, the ceiling's pink and blue
braying a threatening calm,
the patient marks that bored
staidness of the gaze,
prismatic and inclined above him.

The Bolt That Cracked

I did not see it happen, but as one bolt failed,
its release warbled through an intervening
beam and snapped another, also rusted,

which crooked the cradle-plate and twisted
the beam-lip, upsetting in turn the panels
that veered like head-bashers to the concrete.

I heard that and spun as it forwarded,
a crowding fall of scaffold, sixty square feet,
cross-braces, panels, posts, beams, all of it

an impressive un-nuanced cause-and-effect,
men on top with weighted belts
racing to the column heads

as their flooring dived, a swallowing
mess that quaked several stories below.
Bracing the girth of a post

I pivoted from the action
as the Foreman shouted, Heads up,
a last cymbal striking the hip-breadth of my frame.

Quiet heat. What we had done.
The week's worth of falsework
now a pile of shadow under a lack of cloud.

We stood uncomprehending
until it was my side we were staring at.
Certain of a panel, a broad polychromatic bruise,

I was wrong. Shirt-fabric lightly
torn but allocating red. A fourteen footer,
the cradle-plate had rucked

a gash with a graze near my kidneys
deep enough to jam your thumb. I was led
ladder-down to an emerald shack in the mud.

.

At the hospital on a gurney I averted
from a doctor's fluent needle
unevenly underlipping the grin that tongued

at my lower side its flash of fat, his wrist
assured as he yarded the stitching
as if it were a boot he were tightening by a strap—

a svelte tradesman in a chair,
inner thigh a blotted dressing,
a consumptive patient on a stool,

and here, now, this one, hovering
in spacious anaesthetic,
paycheque, gurney or a morgue

all the same to him these days, a mind
of falsework trembling without purpose
implying, where there isn't, a wife

abusing or fussing through televised news,
fatal snipings in Connecticut,
the President's press statement, hoarse

———

sweetnesses as she hectored with a vacuum,
expelled his concealments, annulled
their joint leavings in the sink, the day she left.

·

His sutures demurred, reticent.
His grip lowered along the bar, its cold
metal a piebald of steel and yellow paint.

Old Clip-Clop shouted at a distance,
Brian, newer Foreman from the West,
his stolid shape swooping in a stress,

revolving like a top around a shorter leg—
You're on modified work duty, you shit!
Back to the broom. Or have I got to

throw you off the deck?—Solemn-eyed,
Brian's implicating rictus swerved
to a carpenter's covert shirking in the shade.

And it was quiet here again. Surfaces rimed
with variegated dust. He fronted
with coarse bristles a plume of silica

along even sections of floor. Bass echoings
from above among his milder
sweeps. Air at lower temperature.

Gone four weeks. No word. Primary light
had moved aslant from where he works,
an encroaching total scotoma. Absence. Eclipse.

Remote within the prairies, his people,
he won't speak of what's become of him
except through a half-gall of rum

or bleaker pay-outs of cheap Canadian rye,
saying the least with less under any weather,
until, also quietly, others note the disappearance

of the band on his working hand,
the primitive sparsities of his meals,
his misanthropic moods, throw-downs—

that afternoon Adam tried a joke
about the wife, his making a pass,
with those who knew loosely tense,

with those who didn't sensing a turn,
Adam retracting in his seat
under an instant rancid look—

or his ruckus with Brian, toe-to-toe,
where he damn near cartwheeled
that useless shit sack from the deck,

the slower man surprised but spiking back,
the two shouting as the crew watched,
until they spun in contrary direction,

the subordinate, under his shaded
glasses, surprised even himself as sawdust, rage
and sweat shuddered silently with tears.

•

Quite a shot in the pills, eh? The Foreman
nodded at the stanched puncture at my torso.
Like the others he appraised a lesser wound.

Sure, sure. I scraped with a putty knife
edges of stacked panels shagged
with concrete. But there's worse, I said.

Where are them at, the coilrods? Brian
stared idly through the shoring posts
toward mislaid piles at the fringe of site.

I just seen it, he said. You have to get the rust off em.
With chemical. Before last coffee,
he pointed to a mess of lumber near a stairwell,

Get the rent-a-labourer to put the surplus
two-by's on the headache rack of the truck.
Arright? His look cleared to mine. Azurine.

The pump in the trench. There's no water
comes out of it. Check the hose.
It don't pass mustard. Or water.

Untalkative in a surround of citrus
thought, I waited. Brian,
a lump of empathy he groped at.

About the woman, he said, venting to the floor
a plug of chew. Your head's not in the game.
I get it. But it's her loss, right? Fuck her!

A strafe of midge-flies. No-see-ums aswarm on a breeze.
I dropped the knife and cupped the bites.
That ain't how it is, I said. That ain't what it is.

•

Near the suture,
its mince of bloodpaste, heartmeal, his muscles
seized along his leg and back.

Gale-fingered wind, behind that threaded
mouth, inhaled inert odours
of the room, pulling air through a Tudor keyhole.

He walked through that
aperture on the sweet
silage of rot, shrinking. Amethyst eye of a dime.

He found a man inside who tracked
him hoof by shade through station,
aping in a quiet beyond the lumens

what's bagged or off-centre, a beauty tumour
buried under the linden,
whose speech is the deafening that disrepairs.

He found a man inside with blue scales
glistering in the dark and drew
a knife and drove it up the double's navel.

How his sleeping side throbbed its will in tightness.
His wish that she'd arrive, gravid with crushed violet,
April weather eyes, tear his suture with a fingernail.

Jettisoned

He tries on weeping in the kiln-heavy air.
The trailer's plywood porch granular beneath his heel.

No one else is cupped under
air that's trawling,
this glassed-in agitated earliness.

With a broken hand he pinches his thighs hard as he can
to stimulate a tear that will not rise.

Sluggish cut-throat grief, a fact so hoarse it strakes
through looped intestine, diaphragm, frantic back-fastenings
of an eye, all these scamping, blunted nerves.

Sudden stab of whiskey. Adrenal bloom.

A fact, like infection breaking,
simplifies his throat, quakes the racing muscle.

It recants itself among synapses and fibrous stitchings,
a poison ferrying slow through psychic basins, estuaries
        of the body.

He tries to force it, but the gate creaks.
He rubs away his rheumy eyes.

                    •

On the fourth-floor deck piecing tie-wire, rubble, from
        under the rebar grid,
he sprays oil out of a red can.
It peters brown on the rained-on deck.

Under denim sleeves, this plausible
flesh, she has gone.
A drenched absence, aspirin-cold,
as fixed as mercury or lead. Meters
of rain ploughing in turn.

Who he is
is herniated. Granular,
a glaze of swept water, a split stone.

Rain is as warm as he is.
Yellow and impure
as nectar among browning petals.

He pulls the shaded glasses so he can see.
Twists of foam that stunt his ears.
Dampen and obscure him.

All his hairs, sensors.

Big and black, the storm is a cratering alchemical bowl.

He stares. At the bottom of a cave or a canyon,
cloud-mineral receding to the east.

The black is yawning an entire planet

like the Great Whale that divides and destroys
bleary creation on its rigid plate.

To the west, a slide of rain.

Collapse of an unfortified wall
where all that's built will slide.

Beyond its cankering tone
a sun-spot like a spear.

Thicknesses riven by a spear god.

Prison. Ceiling of a cave or an outlet from a glacier.
Forthright lamp among the disarrayed.

.

He wishes for the clamour of lightning
at the rebar-head of a column.

He waits. Grab-nest of wires in his weakest hand.

He asks that lightning stun him free of hoary fact.
Cauterize knowledge. Flood him under Lethe.
But given thunder, he cries for light.
Misapprehends a movement larger than reckoning.
Mistakes what's thunderous for absence.

.

The storm is burned away.
Bewildered by democratic sun,
he kneels at the wet wrong-angled metal,
fingering garbage. After-end of a task.

Across stacked gear and water-logged timber where the deck
drops in a stomach unprepared, bereaved
by attachment's fuming carcass,
there is someone who will stop his work and speak his name.

Seizures

Keezer, ear in the dirt, cheek peeling in the static August heat,
lifted from the clammy excavation he had dreamed,
the ochre-rooted trench where his hammer,
chalk-line, his carpenter's pencil, slackened in the loam.
Sheets of rain, the rust-coloured spores of ferns—
they quavered and spun—even the
ray of the moon he travelled, all floundered in a voided star.
                                        He had known
telephone numbers, the crutch and wheel of clocks, instruments
for gauging pressure, the soft plain of a woman's wrist.
Now that registry had gone.
Where or what he was, a track of smudge.
            The plateau like an acrid planet, a dull burnt
grey light, the granular cleft between two hills.
There the rilling promise of water, a promontory crop of shade.
Beads of sweat adhered in the matted hair, which he swept back.
        To the right,
an aspen sapling rimpled with want, white as a clipped nail.

                        ◆

He pointed the jackhammer's bit to the pock in the column,
bore his pelvis to the grip, as Larsen watched. Storm clouds
east of the city were loaded parapets, a sheer wall.
The crew argued with scaffolding, beams, a defray of hours,
their wits brawling as they hefted three-by-six-foot panels
or butted the ledgers that propped them up,
urgent for the pump truck, a metric dump of concrete.
They looked on Larsen, who prodded, swayed.
        As Keezer chipped
a column—its layout detrimental, it was placed, poured,

two inches past the slab—Larsen crossed his arms and said,
Put your back into it. Keezer pulled a breath,
yarded the hose that snaked from the air compressor to the jack.
                    Angled at the cured surface
clamping the lever. A bald shock
through his chest. The jack
recoiled, it slammed.
Swiftly retractile dust.
A shaken eyesocket, fat. A piston-
strike that drove
rubble over the drop
eleven floors to the ground.
Shit, Larsen laughed. Heads up!

                              .

Through Keezer's nose the earth-whorled air.
Sulphur? Was it sulphur? The scent
like this passing dream, the minutes—sheets
stacked on sheets of plywood. Across his brain,
its casing, lightness: a tethered hardhat,
fireweed, a crown of stems
through which the jack's hammering
elided, became bolts,
nails, scattering in a bucket—

Here, unafflicted, a man in a raincoat
wearing clean steel-toed boots ripped at the seams,
his gore-tex hood sheening with rain.
Past the column, eleven floors
above the pitted ground, he stood
on nothing. He was
ash, without eyes,
skin the eroded metal of a bronze mask.

Keezer wanted to swear
there were parts of him that could never vanish.
Even when his drill disappeared and his hearing and his rib,
there were parts of him not given to the job,
but his throat shut even for mouthing it.
       No, Laura had the proper words
when it came to a plant or bird
or a guy like him, pinned
in his chest like he was. She pointed out
the California poppies ripening up the cliff,
the twin oystercatchers at the shore,
startled feathered stripes in the moist heat.
       These were days he slept,
when he was unemployed and priceless,
when a green leaf cradled his cheek,
another's hand, and a mouth—
he was thankful for an unpaid sweat,
simply to be warm with Laura on the radiating rock
at the margins of a country that kept on
counting its hours of untapped oil.

Sometimes he heard a dog rushing over stones,
the water's dark brunting weight,
the drone of a plane somewhere overhead,
and he saw her, recklessly still, and so near the plunge.

The horizon flushed with threat, or so he feared.
He felt in the sun's radial orange
an engine's stricken rotor, the glottal
riptide of air charged with a fatal
thousand drops of clean apathetic numbness—
a widespread apparatus spinning in the ventilations,

propelled over hills and wired continents,
repairing the world to its blankness and its fittings—
genitals, microwaves, pills, a jewelled bird,
the fatigued whipping of the bell and its convulsive
dumbfounding, the streamered
nesting of worms, ball-chains, trusses, whose
children shelled and piled in the valley?,
straps, mitre saws, a cabinet of Crown Royal,
Google or government's impound of data,
surveillant, robot, camlock, shackle or sweep,
crowded fuel feeds, combustion, turbines,
the low store of grain, soffits,
lungs, an onion, burgeonings of hunger—

Yes, the sky flushed an orange that could enter
the skin and cut the molecular grain.
            This was the motive of machinery—
built for numbering or splitting stars,
atoms, soils, plastics, books, flags, tendons,
aggregating bytes, bits of glass or dust,
the torque of history on the moment.
            This was the burning place—
the prehistoric sea and its frenzied drowning.
            This was an animal's traded
pelt or an eating site for a fly.
            It revolved like a dial or a cube or a vapour
out of the black that might
veer, without warning, from above.

Here, the lineated darkening sand, the cooling rock,
Laura ten paces ahead. Skimming a foot
in the water as the waves tossed,

she said, I'm hanging
by a thread.

                    ·

There were other revelations—
the white crow on its back with its chest
torn like an envelope, plumage
fringing the cavity
brief as smoke against the raked soil.

When he would wake, nauseous,
staring at the freshly sprayed stipple on the ceiling,
through the variable whiteness he saw
the rippling figure of that bird
and a premonition of water damage—
brown markings on the drywall
someone else would patch—
and he wiped its trace
from his forehead,
wondering from what source
these images came—
carried on a flying
gill or a drowning feather.

            —The next day, or the next,
just the crow's wings remained
and glossed
bits of viscera in the mud.

                    ·

Keezer rested at the broken hill, its alkali facade in long
    diminishment.

Across the ridge the soil sloped. So he slid, denim pocketing
　　with grain,
stalling with his heels as earth roped hotly through his hands—
empty of insect or root—hookleted like fibreglass—
a crawl of silica pluming as he passed—the sky pulseless,
cloudless, hooded by a dulsy centreless sun—he braked short.

　　　　　　The shaft was square and eleven stories deep.
It funnelled darkness, it muted the wrenched
noise of its lowest rooms. He could hear,
barely, the strained efforts below—
they were bunched like ants,
the shirtless men, necks
shining as they shovelled—
scud of steel in the earth.
　　　　　　There were exposed openings
up the side of the pit. Metal jutted
from their cement perimeters. Scaffolds,
beams and posts at higher levels
caught galvanized light—
　　　　　　There was a man with rebar
through his guts, skewered
in the air, his entrails
slick like draining ice—
　　　　　　Another, on a scrap heap,
gaped like a wasp, his head
under grout in a rubber pail—
　　　　　　Farther on, a man, gasping
beneath a capsized pallet of bricks,
shouted as a spider stopped at his brow
where it hooked a thread on a hair.
　　　　　　Mosquitoes, hot sparks of shaved iron,
snarling vagrant dogs or dead air in a tunnel.

At a lower level there was nothing
but a sawhorse layered with dust,
vacant concrete floors extending
without end and starless,
caverns under the burnt white plain.

Then, a shout,
a jet of water at the spade—
it took men at the knees
loping the stairs and floorings.
Between the posts,
a spectre stared across the pit—that man again—
a rusted spike piercing his upper and bottom lips—
every particle of rain about to graze his oiled sleeve
as he watched the water roil and well.
Yes, Keezer also saw it constrict,
a slithering at the curve of darkness,
writhing and grim-plated,
protean at every level.

.

Larsen steadied the freed column as it swung,
hitched to the boom of a crane: a steel rod
through its core near the top, hooked at either end to chain.
He signalled the operator,
bridled down the compressor, detached the hose.
For the next three hours Keezer
chipped at the stump, levelled it to the slab.

Powdered concrete coated the transit of his breath.
His arms tightened. His chemical heart,
a sentimental can of paints,
ruptured a valve: anger, mirth,

wrongly joined with sweetness: Laura's absent
scent over his dusted eyes, his face
trapped in her dark hair,
her laughter
purling under the greased machine's staccato—
as if her mouth were at his ear—
but what's she saying? Sharp
clangour of the tool in his finger-joints,
his wrists—his muscles locked
evenly above the white noise—
his brain and other meat
gangrenous on a rack—
cartilage crowding and crowded. If lightning. If rain.

•

The aspens surged and sank as the storm neared,
a silver moth-dust breach, an abounding pall.
Several crows, a startled hawk with its waning sash,
circled the tower's exposed flank, a rustle
of charcoal, pincer, instinctual, expert—
crows driving for the raptor, now confederate,
desperate, coiling to the distant copse
beyond the cleared contracted earth—
a slender stand of trees in a soil
so clotted with leachates, so
exhausted of solids it became air.

The column levelled, he assembled safety rail,
hedging the slab with two-by-fours, yet
knotted with duplex nails, split,
splintered with re-use, they were junked,
untenable, no resistance in the wood.
He retrieved a skilsaw for the studded ends.
Lumber balanced on his upper leg,

he lifted the guard on the spinning blade.

The heart's twitch in the swelling of his knuckles,
he blundered, his thirst a guttering itch—
it was the doing and the undoing
that happened in the veins—
for he saw the tower was
a gash leaking from the sky,
piped from the sun's
crater to the Earth's.
                    The spectre swung from a beam,
his coat slipping away to a slap of oil.
                    Keezer tried to shout warning
but his panic was tacked
on a crow's blue tongue.

                         •

With his back to the dull accruing dream of hill,
a crosswind lapped with rain,
Keezer worked while men cleared the site,
his arms tired over the skilsaw.
High scent of metal from the disc,
its wheeling—
                    secret of her voice—
bled wildly at the teeth,
his wrists, the red tincture of his eyes—

Tailings

Wading into the lake I rescued
two girls, small as tadpoles—
fixed as twins, in phosphoric dresses.

As I set one on the banked log,
the other, also with your face, slid deeply
back and though I reached into the
brown gulch and pulled and pulled at you
all I drew to the air were twigs, strains, hairs,
knotted on the cracked leg bone
of a bird, phlegmy white feathers or leaves
caked with a century of buried stink
dragged from the world's navel
beneath the troubled tarsands to the north.

There is work for you, my uncle said.
He pointed to the burdened fir
overreaching the log-shed.
There is work, he said, his white hairs
translucent against the fires.
Near the drowning-site where my tool sat
the sky was spotted with stark
citrine burns as if the sky were thread,
were eaten by chemical or nanobyte,
its opal weave eradicated. On my back
my hands sunk a five-pointed web
in the moulded turf. Tumorous blooms
planing slowly and terminally
across the naked blue.
Take heed, my uncle said.
He touched my cheek and vanished.

On the bank to the west the living twin
stood pointing to the tower, saying, Go, go,
incrementally black as I followed
through galleries, lotteries, hotel passages,
until the elevator opened and shut behind us.
The polished haze of aluminum
aged as she aged, marblings of rust,
animal prints, as the air
putrefied in asphyxiating citrine gas.
Go, she said. Go.
And all went dark in her eyes.

In the North Country

His father fell, and it was hard, within the open
A-frame of a barn in the arnica-flowering Peace,
knocked by the sun's ball-peen,
his father's hairless pate a splayed
unfolding butterfly of red
on the toothy rind of the saw—the son
bereft amid the undecked joists.

Clamour of feathers, as if a bird were cooped
in the raftered dark. What his father had seen,
impossibly. An egress of stairs neither had built
that spun: the plywood freshly sanded, sunlit.
The brightening heat where all was shaded,
unapparent, to the son measuring lumber below.

What the neighbours saw when they approached,
parsing from the chest-high wheat. No fallen body.
No blood, no carhartt coat. A rusted hub of nails.

ii.

He was on the shingled roof of a turret. A drop
of rain hurtled from the night like a rock.
Marked his ear on its dart to the stair.
Threaded eight flights of seamless steps.
Dried to nothing. In the basement
an earth tunnel. Each stone in the ropy sheen
like the rusted cheek of a spade or the ball
of an athlete's shoulder. He saw his father's face

preserved in creosote. A rat crossed over it
and it became a clod of till. He stooped
along the crumbled steps until the ceiling sloped,
and flecked mud glistered to dust.
Fluencies of air that swerved. Through a dead
aspen grove a clay trail. Ridge-backed dunes of white.
When he turned, the moon, a cratered coin, had
    slipped away.

Silhouettes

Over the powdered shelf of road, the curbside
descent. Flaps of fire strangled in the quick-
trotted air, a metropolis of dwellers in the dark
shoaled in tunnelled hoodoos, sedimentary bivouacs.
Wrapped in particoloured flannels
men, bunked in monuments of dirt, assembled,
argued, made for the drear hotels trapped astride the rock
or shear-cropped implications of sand. Incalculable fires—
whipping backlit punctures in a screen.
Tracked by emanations, ruminating quorums,
the sparely constellated get-there or evasion.
The scarped distance in lamentations of dust.
We set-to at the cave. We parked the truck,
its canopy bolted. Pisswack buried his device.
I told Pimply Younger at the fire—The days you'd trust
a fair fight, just fists, one on one, are done. Now,
if you're alone, you run. Or you get boot stomped
by five rig-pigs or broke with pipe or knife or worse.

Three of us crossed the berm to an ATCO trailer,
armoured with q-deck, where we could drink.
Languages eddied the benches like smoke
but the coin was the same. Women
with Slavic accents tried the tables
for a meet at Walleyes and Whitetails.
At the plated bar a late-hire labourer
drank a brine with the nub-joint of a human toe
swart and shriven at the base of a glass.
Pimply Younger, Pisswack, and I
played card as moths duped, corroborated

with cased light that looked mildewed and exhumed.
We drained at Pisswack's stealthy two-six of rye,
the hour drugged and anticline, the juke
trolling with a hybrid country tune, a fine lyric
quenched and tempered that we more or less ignored.

Mortar-caked. Hairless. Locum in a corner
whose pawky scar ran like a tear. Heel-clod
drill of ins-and-outs with paper bags.
Cast-out bosses patched with matted gauze.
Locum dragged on a stout cigar—
prime rib, his baked potato, heisted at the deep-fry.
Openly he eyeballed Pisswack. My partner
jawed a shredded hash, its hissing
evisceration of sausage and egg. Locum's scar
lipped-blacker than burnt sugar-cane,
a barbed vendetta riffled with rum. He rose
toward us, trawling with a team,
three small sergeants preparing to throw down,
split faces in the cutlery's limited sheen.
He bent and burped and emptied
his slur of smoke at Pisswack's layered plate.
Implied with breath, pork-link, egg-tremor.
Milliseconds perishable as Pimply Younger
grabbed and flipped the table-top and it began.

Johnny Lightning and the End of the World

He tried to get it right, or at least tried to falsify rightness.
Under the stippled
ceiling within the drywall's whiteness.

His boots gristing at a pebble
he flushed each cabinet, bunted with a ball-peen,
shimming to a hair's width.

Without glide without hinge or handle, drawerless
doorless
things were shaping up.
He covered fractured braces with a countertop.

He marvelled at the smack of contact
glue fuming from the brush.
Careful strokes across a laminate sheet.

Loitering before he plied the marbled slip
he watched the chipboard glisten,
an open sore. Breathed the filtered wad
of tobacco. Tap, flick, of the roach.
                              An ember flaked.
He tried to stop it
butted a calloused palm to that active mote
but it sparked in the glutinous strip and a flame
reeked the rectangular length green and blue.
Braided the entire room.
                              Trim, tile, curtain,
it hopped from shelf to shelf.

He saw the emerging hours with a haze—

a green wave chasing stairwells ceilings
forty-seven stories
Johnny's precinct glumed in smoke—

as rafters forked with flame and sirens failed
it jumped from roof
to roof
embers big as leaves wavering the city—

everything lit up he cried at the phone
its plastic
crumpled, its copper wire spat,

belched, over and under, across the grid—

prisons, power plants, dams, parliaments,
bursting scintillant

rising seas chuting plains east and west
major cities flooded or cooked—

clambering, he viewed the wreckage—

survivors seized the greased and spoiled
rumps of the dead:
                                    until those
bloated sphincters leapt to eat the living
stifling scavengers of air

clamped over the ears below the jaw—

avenues flowerbeds fencelines terraces
became a blotted death-press
pithing roughage, severing brain-stem from spinal cord—

so Johnny threw a spinning carbide blade

a wobbling horseshoe
at every abomination—

charging from the shadow under a chevy's fender

a stray bitch

he severed its arterial clamour—

a jolting taser in the sergant's fist
a stooped grocer
snagging neighbours with a hacksaw—

throwing, Johnny flung he bolted—

gasoline shouting from the jerry cans
and every zealot fried with his placard—

he flabbered he thrashed—

reeled his several discs,
ran empty—

others begged for water
tall shadows
stilted in panic
among the bronzing gusts—

fire in a serpentine trace along the rucked mountains
crackled to the ranger's dugout the priest's hole—

a rage of mice rats mink scattering from the charred
        and sodden
grotto excreting a trail through the heaped mess
crowding after the embers—

he tried to stop it shit he did
his claw slipping for a blow-horn, wireless, spout,

—

but even these fell to pieces in his grip
pages of the phonebook
stuck to his sweat like the cheap ream of a bible—

encircled, alone, he wrung his hands
squat shadow diving
knotted wrists, open throat and whitening hair
smoking weightlessly—
threaded wriggling cornsilk in the flashing air.

Arial

"You could call it the price of prosperity."
Ed Stelmach, Premier of Alberta

"I want my fair share, and that's all of it."
Charles Koch, Chairman of Koch Industries,
sixth-richest man in the world, an oil man

Cuts of tarmac, aspen, lay upturned, where mile-wide road transected
cirques of sand. Sheared referents of hardwood sprigged the sands,
their give of bitumen, terpineol air. From hackled earth, the tar beetle
disclosed itself, the large tar beetle that will grip a knuckle and hold to
it though a man shake and panic before the bite. It overtook disrupt-
ive shelves of sand, an eighty-acre tailings pond crosscut with pipe,
and it outrode contrary understories of air where chafe and pollen
met the snap of its wings. Sharp to the northeast Fort McMurray lay
like a dead spider within the Athabasca. From the pitted abdomen a
floss of traffic reported light and habitual as ants with eggs it pressed
the industrial reach. Furnaces, their cold exteriors, expired a smoke,
crimped wicks a tiered plume that flocked the chamber-heads. The
tar beetle's sclerotic gloss a wandering speck above the inert ponds,
over which its purpose emptied, a mussed iridescent slough at which
to land was silence. Obsidian silent, that wrong dreamtime to enter
into. Waters that were once pleated with oxygen, other ancient feints
of green, lace-work, larvae, stigmatic champagne sun, were now im-
mured with bitumen, an effluent of hydrocarbon, nitrogen, aspirant
sulphur, a fazing lethargy that coalesced in the gas-lit deep, a last of
the first species of fish that now wear asphyxiating polyps in a wreath
around their throats. Their fragments persist under constricts of sun
in country where the waters are endyked and this vast disquiet im-

plemented with declivities, open pits from which three-storied machines tread four-hundred-tonne freights of sand to the neighbouring extraction plants, the skies pistoled with rigs that weltered the graven castes of cloud, refractive smoke through which light degraded and detached. Even distant as-yet-undrilled forests and fens were staked for production, seismic cut-lines along which wolves ran for caribou.

From trailers or the greater offices prudent broad-buckled leaders in faultless hardhats plotted and approved. So they grew, these sectioned encampments rife with spectres, protracted half-lives in bunks or pitch-tents where early ammonia mealed faintly from the mines. These absorptions erased the dream-scent of the sleepers, a force of twenty thousand shoehorned from India, Somalia, Mexico, the Lebanon, wary detachments from Newfoundland, whose ranknesses heated the cubicles. Under the petropolitical shade, lampcameras clocked across the transient char, this indebted city, with beggared Dene or Cree prowling dreamlines dozing under parked cars or backed on drainage ditches. Hastily made hotels faced a sort of darkness, each window a crisis played out mutely, with here, someone crocked in repetitive promises of a screen, those hard agitant lives curated on film, crab catchers, prospectors, scraping dirt for a dime, with there, someone whose hours were spent rooting for porn. Enhoused within these cheapened smoke-stained walls the men marked time, Brad Laberda fried a fist of beef, Vernon Ermentrout ate a wheel of fruit and quietly went blind, the ashen flier-leafed counters aswarm in a throw of pay stubs, tax receipts, tins of tobacco, heaped, heaped inconstantly.

So Highway 63 was a part of this, that patch of road without surcease the people called the Widowmaker, Suicide 63 with its blinker of traffic, truckers with unfazed amphetamine drive whose freight of cable, raw lumber, sol-eclipsing coker ovens, strapped tire piles, clattered on flat-beds at their backs, a retinal rush, a flash of fox on the roadside. The tar beetle clacked through slanting slipdisc dark. It entered an easterly brook and broad yellows and blues rode it through torcs of cloud. Through the days and nights of its eating it detained, that chrononaut. It relented. Winters it stopped altogether. Bred thoroughly in the parapets. Summers it flashed its parts, crossed wetlands, the pyred foglights, laborious upgraders, until it drank subductions of sunlight cold as a trowel, this tar beetle glissing within a bank of spruce burnt umber in the fade where star-sprockets engage with skittering sky-chain, disseveral, that will surge and shock, seize, surrender.

A trailer broke the darkness. Overlooking an empty lot to the north of Edmonton, southeast of High Prairie, late winter runoff in the open ground, it contained three men and a woman. The trailer lay on blocked stilts in the pan of marsh. To the side a cylindrical white propane tank. Further set in the crawling stillness a backhoe with its hydraulic rams and its bowed arm secreted grease from steel nipples some of which were busted or cloyed with grit, lubricant wither-whipping to the ground. Deeper yet an erstwhile dozer, its tread-gear shagged with solid mud. Beside it the high-seated packer with its sheepsfoot drum, inert in the wait and dark. Trenches were stepped as if in imitation of some more ancient work, a foreign convergence of bone or tool. At their centre a spent lakebottom with its lunar-looking clay imprinted with bird feet, half-concealed threes forked and underlapping frays of twig.

The top half of the split tamarack limbs was a leafless yellow. The lower half a rushing shadow. It passed the ice enfeebled there with clay or silt where geese would melt an egress with their bodies. Snow, heaped at perimeters, retained. Spots of compassed fur thereabouts were ravaged dispensations of a rodent caught in its tracks that failed somewhere between the painted stakes sledged in snow and the granulars and gravel, pale delineators of a layout for the future slab. The tar beetle curtailed through this, auricular in declining degrees, a stoop of stairs, an open door.

Inside under tubed light that fell equally over their faces, the tools, the desks, bolts that were turned half a thread too tightly, there were six men, a woman, who waited as the Boss retrieved from his office a broad-capped canister inside which were schematics, neatly foiled leaf. He flattened the rolled print from architectural at a sloped plan table and pressed a steel ruler against it, as if its whiteness were the land, were the throat of an enemy combatant, fine teeth imperial or metric. This'll be the largest pour in the Western provinces, the Foreman said. He shifted one foot to the other like one roped too often and too long. His ears were wasted nubbins from years of frost or sun. The Boss disagreed. On the continent, he said. Diverted from the white print, an overlay of symbol, broken geometry, his gaze was white. Wherever he looked he was snowed in. Always the berms of snow, winters he campaigned against, resistance below, resistance above, and one in the room who would betray him.

Of the gathered reps from other sections whose lateral authority he overrode, it was only the Project Manager he did not consider with contempt. The Area Head, whose station was highest, was debased by a poor grasp of the facts. It was evident he could not take the cold and this degraded his posture in the eyes even of the lowest worker. The Area Head watched warily the genius silence around which each was tethered, each was spoked. We'll complete phase one before the winter, said the Boss at last.

Others did not know or want to know that on his office desk an open fish lay probed upon a tray. Tetrapaks of water were one above the other at the wall. A tool box lay under a script of emergency contacts taped to the cupboard. Through a grilled window at certain removes the excavation was flocked with ash or foreseen in sleek structural steel, a concrete tier that reached in its furnished future toward a word more operative or generative than any tool, a Tetragrammaton untimely and several, picked-for like a stray bone in a parcel of fish. Stormfronts followed flecked bones of creekbeds that fed a river vanished in mosses aeons dead. All such rivers led here, unchartered from the great Athabasca. The scraped till was sheer braille that read of the lakebottom. Earthen insteps were digestibles pale in the pools of shadow. Killdeer fringed the vocable-cut-deep. Incorrect, the Boss amended, Those were snipes. Perishables exhumed there were read from the rock as though by nose. Avian aughts sniffed at among splinters of routed shell. Sprayed placers, staked locates, and lower extants marked with ochre, the plural opening print of paleolithic hands. Shrapnel from some glottal ignition, some original starter fluid few could breathe or guess. Barbed crop. Nail-pinner. Prier. Instructions from an alphabet sacrosanct, on fire, a letra brought low. Some of these stones broke open under the machine-tread in a cloud-flash, burdens of migraine powdering in moonlight, destroyed in the air but momentarily glimpsed against the face. The world's before-and-after a brief silage bestirred within a cloud of rock or tweezered from a tumour or a fin, each *fractura melisma* destroyed as it was gathered, a unit of vigour like a unit of fuel, bitumen escalade of exhaust, spoil piles, the great buckets of land burnt through the furnace-mouth, syllables of Tetragrammaton shucked from the source but never assembled entire. I will relent, he said amid smoke and steam from his highest lookout. Gatherings of his men were like ant colonies tapped through the brain by revivifying spores that steered their hosts toward an end-game of succession. Himself was an incubation, disarticulate and hoarse, as he reckoned every foil, counterfoil. In the dark he saw gradations of darkness.

Closure

The parapets were rolling with silica. The wind that whipped at masonry made puppetry of the dust under the tall lamps—uniform cinderblocks, deadlocked byways, barrels of dustbane that reeked of canola and were clawed through, a troved beguilement breaking greasily in hand—a draught that swerved the lip of passages that suggested other entrances, overfull storage units in decline, segregated lunch rooms with their strew of pulp, all in a rubric of turning that led to the first passage. The tower the men had built overshadowed the outbuildings and patrol-going walls that surrounded it: concentric rings of concrete punctuated with surveillance cages, narrow little cupolas of five paces. Violets grew in the cracked lengths of tube, sorted but ignored. The men were standing outside that last segment of the last wall they had poured, which was the last wall they were to pour: at the form-head rain was driving dimples into the concrete as it stiffened. The wall was higher than the men by a great height but dwarfed by the tower behind it. The men were waiting because they wanted to walk away and they didn't any of them want to be the first. You must never be the first, one admitted.

In the fate of builders and their bosses there came a point at which the lower rungs of labour packed up their gear, a crescent wrench, a gooseneck, a cat's claw—plethora of trial or humour—and got on to the next site, the next, the next. But at this point there were also those whose walkabout continued. A stifled barbeque with a hornet's nest asleep under the hood, the racked vats of remover, the clicking abide of beetles in the broken joins, he passed them by. Automatic doors registered with a scan around him. In this panopticon the Boss could drill through nothing with his power for it was made by him and that other one who re-enforced his imagination for a price. The trades withdrew, but he remained. He was circumspect, crossing a laboratory.

He didn't understand the rove of horse's hair near the electrical room, those skittering computations that reached the ceiling and flanked the walls. Workers had complained of that machinery clouding their heads: it was fractious, that drone, a white mould that furred through every thought. They were afraid to open their mouths because they believed their own water might draw an arc, a total reprimand that might burst a limb or stop a heart.

The Boss couldn't reason the piquant scent that broiled at the grates, sterile places, a whiff of bilge, strut of lemon, daubed understories that unpredictably changed. In other sections these traces gave way to a distortion in lockers or drains: of porcelain rattling as if it were stacked saucers in a ship's kitchen, rocky with the black waves, needling an active pass; of a sunburnt's practiced shout from his bicycle, *helado, helado,* a nauseous cantaor waking the stray dogs in that market of pissmongers and goats; of a radio's mesmeric rustle where there can be no radio... *He is exiting the East Wing...He is listening, ear cupped, at the intake... overcome with regret, he is ashen, that New Year's Eve...where it was lost, a seam...* a script of news anxiously dreeped through a ductwork or a stairwell like a bit of gravel. The Boss walked these cul-de-sacs as if they were, were what exactly?, the fretwork of an appetite, a nubile imagination that could build all of this, with strictly the assigned material, with strictly less. The tower and its outliers would seem a chamber of echoes where amphoras were turbulent with bodies or honey was steepled into a wagon's jostling crate-hold of clay jugs. Men were grunting or answering Russian as they dug by the fistful that great canal or blood-furrow, perekovka, their spines a tested undergird. Water ran through the swale as expected but with ephemera that gainsaid the place or time: a condor feather, a Venus figure, a green balloon with a clown's sawed-off talon mummified to the nylon tassel. The Boss couldn't shake the suspicion he had intercepted vague, secret signage. This wasn't, it wasn't right. He was archivist, that hoarder of secrets: no one knew as he did the weal and camber of that place, it was his, he had paid for it. He swallowed his dose of white pills. He felt as though he'd done all this before, in starker uniform, graver emblem.

In the winkling mortician's light of that walkabout he bore to the outer circle, a last wall of concrete that half-blocked the moon. He stood with his Foreman, the Safety Officer, the Project Manager, and the last men, who checked their pouches. A wreath, like rotten fish, from a white bag. The carpenters can go, he said. They sprayed their coveralls and shovels with a hose. They scuffed the gravel as they gave the uppers, and him, a wide pass. Their shadows ebbed toward the far egress, where they weren't seen again. The Area Head was late: he had not called. The Boss was unsurprised, he didn't care: that man an enemy and worse, an incompetent. I don't know as that's necessary, he said. One of the lampstilts cut out and in, blacklisting. The Foreman asked about a misinformation that had gotten his way. The Boss drew from a cigarette. My expectation is…Yes and no, he said. The moon was gradually erased. The formwork darkened, its strata of joists and stringers. Be that as it may…the Boss stopped. He saw the glimmer of movement at the peripheral, on the wall, as if a reptile were riffling from a brick. No, he said. The tang of a snapped tie prefigured that metal-wreak of torsion: sleeper's burst, a blow-out. The men were backlit by industrial casts as if by a white yawn of flame, the devouring bright with its indentations of anguish. A vaunt of concrete like an ocean, like a slow ocean, overrode them. Their several forms spired like devils of dust, smallness that wheeled and stuttered, but the Boss refuted in place. I will be appeased, he stared. The wave, at large, engulfed them each with silence.

Prologue for the Age of Consequence

The tower begins in the slaughterhouse hours
of Troy's burning-after morning
beyond the mosquito-netting screen
where throats boil and bloom
under the mercantile heat-mad flies.
Begins in the meteor-trail
where the gilded leader falls.
When Descartes isolates stone from stone,
churches ossify the dome,
these flowers frost and fade.
Begins when banks fix interest,
revolution, liberty's sluggish stove-light
squinting off and on and off.

We deplanted currencies, tribes. Machines began
to count even the motes of the soul
adrift in the microwavable
avatar country of the digital.
Googling the gloss, the teflon-
photographic
ping that might
or might not prove the spirit,
we upheeled currencies, tribes, etherneting
shadowstructures, circumscribing rights
through a fibre-optic hub.

So the tower plumbed, it spired. How-or-by-whatever.
FOX reports by wire that proper-
minded citizens can trust in common sense, if-
by-consensus, if-by-God.

Forty stories, eighty, or a hundred, the tower's
base crusts and clogs. At such height,
pressures redisperse—glass-panes
sucked out, not in, as hurricanes hit—
girders twisted back and forth
like a door-handle's rattled turning. We say
its columns weren't fire-rated. We say
a lot of things, the impossible happening
if a story insists: our Lady streaked with oil, blood;
your brother come to from the clay;
girders melted—hundreds of concrete
stories dissolved—free-falling,
purified at the teleprompter,
thermite smudged in the holy smoke.

Across this vagrant city, the programmatic
cyber-techné plain,
a stooped figure carries news.
The bedsheet hackled at his neck
conceals his forearm's flaking and corruption.
Perhaps we've known it,
burning these many lives.

The tower will erupt. Blacken
Detroit, New York, Madrid, Montreal.
The Government clone itself
as banks fail or feint and architects re-write law.

The commonwealth
gimletted.

So much siphoned. Grain zeroing worldwide.
Aquifers, rivers. This unexpected Age.
The tower, fulgent with suck.

Notes

In the opening lines of "In the North Country," "the arnica-flowering Peace" refers to the Peace, a colloquial name for the territory near the Peace River, also a city by that name, in northern Alberta, Canada.

In later stages of this manuscript I read Andrew Nikiforuk's *Tar Sands: Dirty Oil and the Future of a Continent*. No one else has in such exacting detail scrutinized the oil industry's withering influence in Canada and the United States. His book provided factual grounding for the prose poem "Arial." If there are errors, they are mine.

The title *Prologue for the Age of Consequence* is derived in part from the title of a document, produced jointly by the Center for Strategic and International Studies and the Center for a New American Security, called *The Age of Consequences: The Foreign Policy and National Security Implications of Global Climate Change*, an austere forecast for the next hundred years. Contributors include experts in climate science, foreign policy, national security, oceanography, history, and political science, among them Nobel Laureate Thomas Schelling, and senior American political advisors such as former CIA Director James Woolsey, former Chief of Staff to the President John Podesta, and former National Security Advisor to the Vice President Leon Fuerth.

Acknowledgements

Many thanks to the editors of the following publications: *Poetry Ireland Review*, *Hazlitt*, *This Magazine*, *Prism International*, *Vallum*, and the *Times Colonist*. I am grateful to the following for their financial support: the Canada Council for the Arts, the University of Victoria's Department of Writing, and the Writers' Trust of Canada. A selection of poems from this manuscript won the Bronwen Wallace Award in 2011. My thanks to the staff at the Writers' Trust for their attendant generousity, and also to the judges.

Immense gratitude to my editor, Sara Peters, for her faith in the work and her thorough interrogation of the poems. Lasting thanks to Lorna Crozier for editing an earlier draft of this manuscript and for her mentorship and friendship. You were the very best of teachers. Thanks also to Tim Lilburn for asking important questions and for conversation that was always, even where casual, insightful. Thanks to Lorna Jackson, Steven Price, Carla Funk, and John Barton. I am deeply thankful for the advice and friendship of Anne-Marie Turza, Allison Blythe, and Melanie Siebert.

For her measureless support and unswerving confidence, I thank Denise Yeo. For various indescribable contributions, some of them vaguely editorial, but all of them profoundly affectionate, I am indebted to Chelsea Rushton, Eliza Robertson, Jessie Jones, Liam Sarsfield, Vincent Colistro, Stephanie Warner, Danielle Janess, Simone Littledale, Britt Jay Bates, Susan Sanford Blades, Deborah Willis, Mike Bond, and Meaghan Hume. Your personal and professional camaraderie means so much to me. Thank you.

Endless thanks to my family. To my mother, Amy, for her love of reading. It all began there. To my father, Vern, whose working life is an example, in its discipline and reach, and whose small encouragements were very large in fact. I love you both. Thanks also to the Penners, the Schubels, and Ron Smith and Virginia Hallonquist.

I am grateful to Travis Swicheniuk, Iain MacLean, and Sam Azooz for their fraternity and reliability through many perilous moments on job sites.

For their assistance in making this book, I thank Kelly Joseph, Laura Repas, Damian Rogers, Sarah MacLachlan, and the rest of the staff at Anansi. I'm grateful also to Brian Morgan, who designed it, and Peter Norman, who proof-read it. Thanks also to Jared Bland, who first acquired the manuscript.

Photograph © Chelsea Rushton

Garth Martens' writing has appeared in *Poetry Ireland Review, Hazlitt, This Magazine, The Fiddlehead, Prism, Vallum, Grain,* and *The Malahat Review.* In 2011 he won the Bronwen Wallace Award for Emerging Writers. He has worked eight years in large-scale commercial construction. *Prologue for the Age of Consequence* is his first book. He lives in Victoria, British Columbia.